HERO JOURNALS

Ramesses II

Richard Spilsbury

Raintree is an imprint of Capstone Global Library Limited, a company incorporated in England and Wales having its registered office at 7 Pilgrim Street, London, EC4V 6LB – Registered company number: 6695582

To contact Raintree:
Phone: 0845 6044371
Fax: + 44 (0) 1865 312263
Email: myorders@raintreepublishers.co.uk
Outside the UK please telephone +44 1865 312262.

Text © Capstone Global Library Limited 2014
First published in hardback in 2014
The moral rights of the proprietor have been asserted.

Edited by Adam Miller, Charlotte Guillain, and Claire Throp
Designed by Richard Parker and Ken Vail Graphic Design
Original illustrations © Capstone Global Library Ltd 2014
Illustrated by Stathis Petropoulos
Picture research Tracy Cummins
Production by Victoria Fitzgerald
Originated by Capstone Global Library Ltd
Printed and bound in China by Leo Paper Products Ltd

ISBN 978 1 406 26569 9
17 16 15 14 13
10 9 8 7 6 5 4 3 2 1

British Library Cataloguing in Publication Data
Spilsbury, Richard
Ramesses. – (Hero journals)
932'.014'092-dc23
A full catalogue record for this book is available from the British Library.

Acknowledgements
We would like to thank the following for permission to reproduce photographs: Akg p. 19 (IAM/akg); Alamy pp. 13, 26 (© Peter Horree), 35 (© Art Directors & TRIP); Art Resource, NY pp. 9 (© Erich Lessing), 15, 18 (© Werner Forman), 16 (© The Trustees of the British Museum), 31 (© Eileen Tweedy), 36 (© James Morris); Bridgeman Art Library pp. 11 (© Christie's Images), 34 (© Giraudon), 37 (© Tarke), 7; Corbis p. 28 (© A. W. Cutler/National Geographic Society); Getty Images pp. 20 (Patrick Aventurier/Gamma-Rapho), 24 (Prisma/UIG), 33 (Ariadne Van Zandbergen), 39 (DEA PICTURE LIBRARY); National Geographic Stock p. 38 (O. Louis Mazzatenta); Shutterstock pp. 4 (© Zsolt Horvath), 30 (© Dmytro Korolov), 32 (© Przemyslaw Skibinski);

Design elements supplied by Shutterstock (© R-studio), (© Pavel K), (© Picsfive), (© karawan).

Cover photograph of a statue of Ramses II at Nubiano Museum reproduced with permission of Corbis (© Sandro Vannini).

Contents

I am Ramesses the Great

My bones ache and it is agony to eat because my mouth is full of sores. The doctors and servants who fuss over me can do little to ease my discomfort. I am 90 years old, and I know that my earthly body is fading fast, but this doesn't matter to me because I am Ramesses the Great. I have ruled over Egypt for more than 60 years and accomplished more than my father.

Ancient Egypt

Around 3100 BC, the many separate little kingdoms along the River Nile were joined to form one long, thin country ruled by one king, or pharaoh. Before Ramesses II came to power in 1279 BC, pharaohs had ruled Egypt for nearly 2,000 years.

My stone statues adorn my kingdom and remind all of my greatness.

My successes

I can look back upon my long life with pride. During my successful reign, I made our great kingdom of Egypt a bigger, richer place. I built more monuments, won greater battles, and fathered more children than any other pharaoh! My tomb is ready in its rightful place in the Valley of the Kings, and I know my name will live on, long after I have joined the other gods in the afterlife.

These hieroglyphs spell my name – ruler of all Egypt. I had it carved on all the temples in the Nile Valley!

Document it!

When you're planning a journal, take some time to decide how you want to order it. Do you want it to follow from past to present as Ramesses does, or do you want to organize it by themes, such as music, sport, friends?

My early years

I was born to greatness. I have inherited my father's flame-red hair. This is unusual in Egypt, so I was marked from the very start of my life as special. I was born in 1303 BC. My father is Seti I, pharaoh of Egypt, and my mother is Queen Tuya. I am named after my grandfather, Ramesses I, another great leader.

Ramesses I

Ramesses I was named Paramessu at birth. He was a soldier like his father, who rose rapidly in the ranks and grew close to the pharaoh, Horemheb. Horemheb had no children, so when he died he made Paramessu ruler. In 1292 BC, in his fifties, Paramessu took the throne as Ramesses. He died 16 months later.

My grandfather took his name Ramesses I after the great sun god Ra (left).

Growing up

My home is the royal palace in Memphis on the delta of the River Nile. I love sports such as archery, swimming, and horse riding, and I am very skilled at these. I am also learning maths, hieroglyphs, science, and other important subjects from the very best tutors. I learn fast, but I'm often told off for playing tricks on the priests!

River Nile

The River Nile helped to make Egypt rich. Fishermen caught fish from the river, and every year it flooded and washed thick mud onto the dry land around it. Farmers grew vegetables, corn, and other crops in this rich, dark soil. They built channels to carry river water to farms to help plants grow and for animals to drink.

Egypt is hot and dry but the River Nile brought water and life. These people are harvesting crops next to the Nile.

Training for greatness

My father is training and testing me to prepare me to be pharaoh. He sets me many challenges. I have caught and killed a fierce, wild bull. I survived alone in the harsh, open desert, where the Sun burns your skin by day and the cold chills your bones at night. Today, I had to handle poisonous snakes! So far, I have passed every challenge.

Seti I

Seti I reigned from 1290 to 1279 BC. He fought many battles to win back lands lost in previous years. He opened a rock quarry at Aswan to provide stone for magnificent building projects. He was named after Set, a red-headed god.

This carving on the walls of the Seti I temple at Abydos shows Seti I and I looking at the list of names of pharaohs who ruled before us.

A great honour

Today is a great day. I am 14 years old, and my father has made me Prince Regent. This means I will rule all Egypt with my father. I have risen quickly in his esteem. At the age of 10, he made me captain of the army. I learned to lead the soldiers and gained experience in battle skills and strategy. By the age of 12, I fought my first battle and proved that I will be a great warrior. This honour is my reward.

> "The All-Lord [Seti] himself made me great, while I was a child, until I reigned ... I was installed as eldest son, as hereditary prince upon the throne of Geb [the earth god] ... [He, Seti, said] 'Crown him as king, that I may see his beauty while I live with him' ..."
>
> Ramesses II

9

Monuments and palaces

As Crown Prince, I have many duties. I oversee the quarry in Aswan, where workers cut black granite. I check and approve their work on my father's building projects, such as the magnificent statue of him for the temple of the god Osiris at Abydos. I design my own monuments, too, and order statues and treasures for inside the temples. Our stone temples will last forever!

Temples for the gods

The Egyptians believed that to keep their empire going, they had to keep a magical connection with the gods. The pharaoh was seen as the link between people and the gods, so the Egyptians built magnificent temples where they worshipped the pharaoh and, through him, the gods.

A palace of my own

Now that I am 15, my father has given me my own luxurious palace. I live here with my first wife Nefertari, who has given me my first son. My second wife, Isetnofret, has given me another. We live well. We dine on fish from the Nile flavoured with spices bought from Asia and the Mediterranean and eat fruits such as figs, dates, and pomegranate. We hold grand parties, and musicians, dancers, and acrobats entertain us.

Nefertari

Little is known about Nefertari, but she became an important queen. Ramesses II wrote love poems about Nefertari, whom he loved dearly. He treated her as an equal, which was unusual in those times. He asked her for advice, and she stood by his side at ceremonies and at court, where important decisions were made.

Nefertari means "beautiful companion" — and that is what she is to me.

Early battles

Now I ride by my father's side in many important battles. Our aim is to win back land taken by Nubian and Hittite armies. The Hittites have been a thorn in Egypt's side for many years. Before my father and I ruled, the treacherous Hittites stole land that was rightfully Egypt's in North Syria. My father and I fight bravely to regain control of this region.

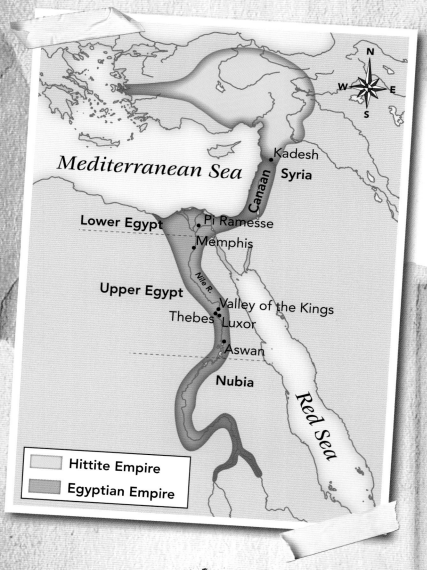

The Hittites are to the north and the Nubians in the south of our region.

Document it!

It's fun to use maps in a journal. You can use them as a background to photos or notes, or mark the places you stayed or routes you took on a holiday. You could also include those maps you get at theme parks and zoos as memories of days out.

Nubian treasures

I am now 22 years old. I have just returned from Nubia, where we fought the fierce Nubians, who were trying to steal our land. I killed many enemies with my bow and arrow, fired from my speeding chariot. My two young sons — aged three and four — watched proudly, driven in chariots that rode close behind me. In victory, I sat upon a throne while a procession of Nubians brought me offerings such as food, animals, gold, ostrich feather fans, and other treasures.

After the Nubians are defeated, they lay their treasures before me as their conqueror.

Nubian gold

Egyptian pharaohs wanted to control Nubia so they could take gold from the mines there. Gold was highly treasured by Egyptians, as they believed the skin and bones of the gods were made of gold. They used gold to make jewellery, headdresses, and fabulous treasures for palaces and temples.

Becoming pharaoh

It is 1279 BC and my beloved father, Seti I, is dead. We must wait 70 days for his soul to pass to heaven and for the embalmers to preserve his body, so he can live on in the afterlife. Then we will bury him in the Valley of the Kings and I will be confirmed as pharaoh in Thebes.

Mummification

After a corpse was washed, embalmers removed the brain via the nose using a hook. Then they cut out internal organs and put these into special jars. The body was covered with salt and dried out for 40 days. It was then stuffed to give it shape again. It was adorned with gold, jewels, and charms to ward off evil and then wrapped in linen bandages.

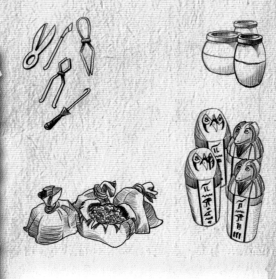

We Egyptians preserve our dead by mummification.

The funeral begins

We held my father's funeral today. Queen Tuya, Nefertari, and I led a procession of boats to the Valley of the Kings. Then I led the walk to the tomb, followed by priests carrying the gold coffin and servants carrying furniture and gold. In the tomb, we held ceremonies to prepare my dead father for the afterlife. Afterwards, the tomb doors were sealed and I became king.

Queen Tuya

Tuya was the daughter of an officer. Her first son by Seti I died; Ramesses was her second. After Seti I died, Tuya took the official role of King's mother to help Ramesses in his first years as ruler.

One funeral ritual was to touch the parts of the face to allow the dead to see, hear, eat, and drink in the afterlife.

15

Royal duties

Last night, Nefertari and I prayed at Karnak temple in Thebes, home of the god Amon. I vowed to uphold the laws of Maat, the god of justice and order. This morning, after washing carefully, I dressed in white and gold. I have a bull's tail on the back of my kilt as a symbol of power. As I sat on the throne and my mother chanted my name, the weight of my new responsibilities and power hit me.

The two crowns represent his rule over Upper and Lower Egypt.

The fake beard shows his status as a living god (Egyptians believed gods had beards).

The crook and stick show his power over his people.

This statue of Ramesses II shows the symbols of Egyptian pharaohs.

The Festival of Opet

One of the first celebrations of my new rule was the Opet festival, celebrating Amon, king of the gods. I travelled to Luxor Temple with the gold-decorated statue of Amon, followed by priests, musicians, dancers, and singers. Crowds gathered to catch a glimpse of the god's statue, usually hidden from their eyes in the temple. In ceremonies in the heart of the temple, I was given the power of Amon and renewed my right to rule.

Amon is considered to be the god of kings and king of gods!

Egyptian gods

Ramesses had a huge impact on religion. King Akhenaton (1353–36 BC) made Egyptians worship only his personal god, Aton, instead of many gods. Ramesses worshipped many gods who had different roles. This form of worship also established the pharaoh as a true son of the gods.

My family

Ordinary men take only one wife, but as pharaoh, I am expected to have more. I have taken eight royal wives and many, many concubines.

Of my eight queens, Nefertari is and always will be my favourite. She rules by my side. My wives have given me many treasured children, and they are truly a great blessing in my life.

Merenptah was Ramesses's 13th son. He eventually became pharaoh after Ramesses's death.

Life expectancy

In ancient Egypt, a mother would be very lucky if half of her children lived to be adults. Many children died from diseases that we can cure with medicines today, but that weren't discovered then. Ramesses had 96 sons and 60 daughters, but 12 of his older sons from his chief queens died before he did.

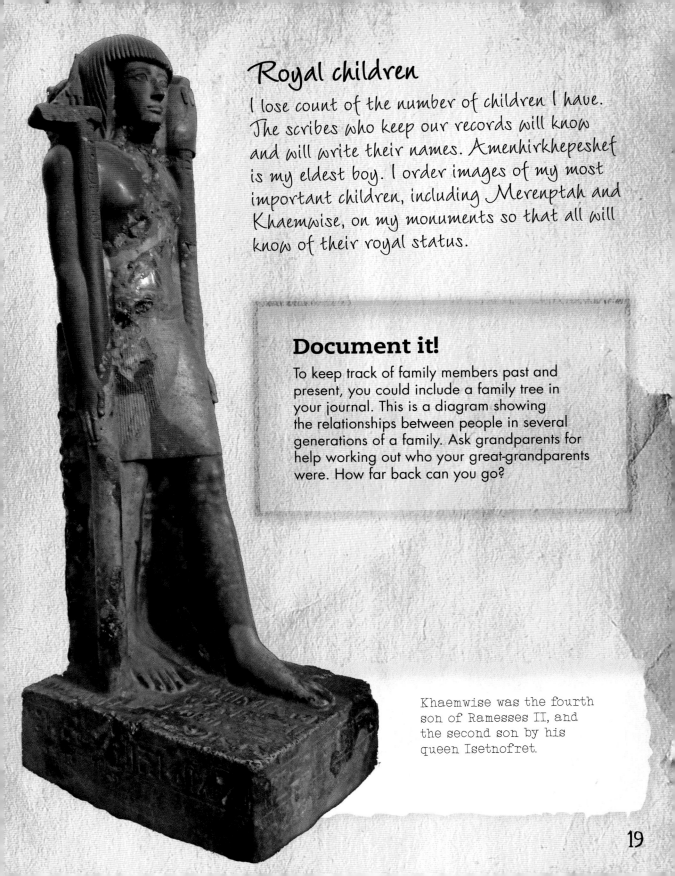

Royal children

I lose count of the number of children I have. The scribes who keep our records will know and will write their names. Amenhirkhepeshef is my eldest boy. I order images of my most important children, including Merenptah and Khaemwise, on my monuments so that all will know of their royal status.

Document it!

To keep track of family members past and present, you could include a family tree in your journal. This is a diagram showing the relationships between people in several generations of a family. Ask grandparents for help working out who your great-grandparents were. How far back can you go?

Khaemwise was the fourth son of Ramesses II, and the second son by his queen Isetnofret.

Making Egypt greater

Since my first years as pharaoh, I have set about making Egypt greater to show the world that I am a force to be reckoned with. Now I have built a splendid new capital city in the north, named after me. Pi Ramesse is close to the borders of my enemies. From here, I can lead my armies to win back land, and bring back prisoners, money, and treasures, to make Egypt richer and more powerful.

Pi Ramesse means "House of Ramesses", and the city was about 96 kilometres (60 miles) north-east of modern-day Cairo, on the banks of the River Nile.

Pi Ramesse

Pi Ramesse had a population of around 300,000 people. It had flowering trees, lakes, towering statues of Ramesses, and even a zoo! Ramesses' palace here sparkled with gold and precious blue stones, such as lapis lazuli and turquoise.

Weapons of war

For war we need weapons. I have ordered swords, shields, spears, and axes to be made in the new factories in Pi Ramesse. My workers build fine warships and many new chariots that are lighter and faster than any we have used before. They can build 250 chariots in two weeks. My soldiers train relentlessly. Soon we will be ready to fight.

Sea people

Ramesses' Egypt faced enemies in all directions, even from the sea. Pirates such as the Sherden people attacked and robbed ships and villages around the Mediterranean coast. Ramesses sent armies to defeat them and then forced the prisoners to fight for him in his own battles.

The Battle of Kadesh

It is 1274 BC, and warships loaded with horses, soldiers, and weapons followed my golden barge from Pi Ramesse to attack Kadesh in the north, which the Hittites have regained. I have 20,000 men at my command, divided into four groups, each named after an Egyptian god: Amon, Ra, Ptah, and Set. I led the first group to the city. We captured two Hittites who had come to spy on us. They told us their army was far off, but they lied. The Hittites had laid a trap and were just across the river, ready to attack.

> *"The 2,500 spans of chariotry, in whose midst I was, became heaps of corpses before my horses."*
>
> Taken from the walls of the Ramesseum

Under fire

As if from nowhere, Hittite King Muwattalli charged at us with hundreds of chariots. Arrows flew at us from all sides. Many of my men were killed or fled in fear. The god Amon gave me the courage to race alone on my chariot against the enemy! My courage inspired my men to follow. Then my remaining forces arrived and surprised the Hittites. Together, we killed many of the enemy and chased many others into the river.

The truth about Kadesh

On his return from battle, Ramesses ordered scribes, artists, and stone carvers to advertise his great bravery everywhere. The truth of Kadesh was different. Ramesses had walked into a trap, lost thousands of men, failed to recapture Kadesh, and promptly withdrew far to the south!

When I ride into battle,
my pet lion races
alongside my chariot.

Sieges and strategy

Since the Battle of Kadesh, the Hittites have been encouraging rulers in neighbouring countries and within Egypt to defy me. My armies storm their walled cities in a blaze of fury to show them Egypt's mighty power. At Dapur, my soldiers scaled the city's high walls on ladders. Archers circled in their chariots, firing on any enemies that dared to show their heads above the walls. Officers smashed down the gates with heavy axes.

The Egyptians used ladders to get over the walls and towers of the city of Dapur in Syria.

Document it!

Much of the information we have about Ramesses comes from ancient paintings of real events. Use photos to document your life in your journal, too. Put dates and captions on them so people will know what happened, and when.

The power of plotting

I fight the Hittites with strategy, too. Urhi-Teshub should be their leader, but his corrupt uncle Hattusili III stole his throne. Now Urhi-Teshub has escaped and come to Egypt. I welcomed him to our court. I know that this will anger Hattusili and make it hard for him to rule. Many Hittite people still want Urhi-Teshub to be their king, and now he is here, they will call for his return. Ha!

Hittite kings

The Hittite king Muwattalli had died several years after Kadesh. His son Urhi-Teshub was to succeed him, but Muwattalli's younger brother Hattusili seized the throne and banished his nephew to Syria. Urhi-Teshub escaped his Hittite minders and fled to Egypt. Ramesses refused Hattusili's demands that he be returned to him.

Hittite warriors were strong and carried a range of weapons.

Peace with the Hittites

Hattusili was furious that I would not return Urhi-Teshub to him, but he hasn't enough men to fight Egypt. So, we agreed to make a peace treaty. For two years, messengers have been carrying versions of the treaty between the Hittite capital, Hattusa, and Pi Ramesse, which is a one-month journey each way. At last now, in 1259 BC, we have agreed and signed it.

The treaty of 1259 BC was the first international peace treaty in the world. It was written in the international language of the day, Akkadian.

> "Reamasesa (Ramesses II), the great king, king of the country of Egypt, shall never attack the country of Hatti to take possession of a part [of this country]. And Hattusili, the great king, king of the country of Hatti, shall never attack the country of Egypt to take possession of a part [of this country]."
>
> From the treaty

The peace treaty

The treaty has brought calm. In it, we agreed the borders between our two territories, and not to attack each other's lands. Everyone is celebrating. Temples are decorated and offerings are made to the gods. The name Ramesses the Great echoes across all Egypt. My marriage to one of Hattusili's daughters, Princess Maathorneferure, will seal the bond between our two peoples.

King Hattusili III

Hattusili was a very sick child, but he survived and became chief supporter of his older brother Muwattalli, who became king after their father's death. Even before Muwattalli's death, Hattusili had proved his military skill by driving enemies out of Hittite lands in the north and taking control there.

Land of temples

Now, in these years of peace and prosperity after war, I turn my attention back to building mighty monuments to the gods so they will protect our land. To get the quantities of stone I need, I often destroy former pharaohs' monuments. Some think this is overstepping my power, but they never dare to complain. At Karnak, I continue work on the Hypostyle Hall begun by my grandfather and father. Only I and important priests can stand under its forest of high stone columns.

The pillars in the Hypostyle Hall at Karnak were about 21 metres (69 feet) high!

Building techniques

Architects worked out complicated designs for temples. Boats carried huge stones from quarries to ships on the Nile, and then slaves and workers dragged them from the river to the building sites. It took so long to build these monuments that Ramesses had a village built for the workers at Thebes.

Cartouches

Whenever Ramesses built or improved and repaired temples and monuments, he made sure they commemorated him by having his own cartouche added to them. A cartouche is a name written in hieroglyphs enclosed in a loop, like a nameplate.

Tombs

I have also ordered the building of a vast underground tomb at the Valley of the Kings. It has over 100 separate rooms cut into the rock. These will be for my children when they die. To foil the thieves who try to rob our burial places of their treasures, we are making many corridors that lead into dozens of different chambers. That should confuse them!

Ramesseum

I ordered work to begin on the Ramesseum shortly after I came to the throne, but it has taken 20 years to complete. This temple is a record of my reign and it is where I will be worshipped after death. Scenes from the famous Battle of Kadesh and other events are painted and carved on its walls. The base of my gigantic statue weighs more than 1,000 tonnes and is admired in the inner court by the public on festival days.

Temple life

Temples were not just places of worship. They were the centre of life in a town. Craftsmen worked there making objects for the temple. Farmers had to pay a tax to the temple. Every day, they brought in contributions of food and meat to be counted. These helped to pay the priests who looked after the temple and its grounds.

Giant statues of Ramesses II flank the entrance to the Ramesseum.

Recording a life

I come to check on the progress of the Ramesseum and stay in my palace here. Thousands of people work here, including priests, soldiers, craftsmen, and labourers. There is a school where scribes are trained. Once they have mastered their task, they will help to fill the magnificent temple library in the Ramesseum called the House of Life. It will have 10,000 papyrus scrolls about my life.

Ramose was a scribe who worked during the reign of Ramesses II.

Scribes

Scribes recorded information for the pharaoh, government, priests, and officials in Egyptian courts. They wrote in ink on papyrus (a type of paper made from sedges from the Nile delta) and carved into stone. Ramesses trained as a scribe to complete his education in Memphis.

31

Abu Simbel

My colossal sun temple at Abu Simbel is a fantastic achievement. Unlike other temples built from blocks, it is carved into the sheer, rocky face of a cliff. There are four giant statues of me at the front — each weighing as much as 170 elephants! These strike fear into the hearts of Nubians and all others entering Egypt from the south.

The giant statues of Ramesses (one is missing its head today) at Abu Simbel are 20 metres (65 feet) tall!

Statues for posterity

Ramesses II had more giant statues of himself erected than any other pharaoh before him, to ensure that his name lived on. Inscriptions were carved deeply into structures so that they could not be easily destroyed or removed by succeeding empires.

Ramesses claimed to have built Abu Simbel to honour the sun gods, but these statues of Osiris have the features of Ramesses II himself.

A sacred place

My sacred temple holds a magnificent secret. It is carved so that twice a year, on the days of my birth and coronation, sunlight shines down the three connected halls that are carved 56 metres (185 feet) deep into the mountain and lights up the shrine hidden there. The sunlight shines upon me and two sun gods, but leaves the statue of Ptah in darkness. Ptah is a god of the underworld and darkness, who sits by our side.

Document it!

Ensure you will be remembered in the future, too! Write your journal in pencil first so you can correct mistakes. Then write over it with permanent ink that will not fade over time. Or type it up on a computer and save it there.

A tomb for Nefertari

It is the saddest time of my life. It is 1255 BC, and my beautiful Nefertari is dead. She was only in her late forties. I am lost without her. I have built her the most spectacular tomb in the Valley of the Queens. The best painters worked on her resting place, for only they could truly reproduce her dazzling beauty. This is how the world shall remember her — in long, white robes, jewels, and a headdress of gold.

Nefertari was buried in the most beautiful tomb in the Valley of the Queens.

"My love is unique – no one can rival her, for she is the most beautiful woman alive. Just by passing, she has stolen away my heart."

Ramesses II

A house of eternity

I instructed the painters to fill Nefertari's House of Eternity with images of the gods assisting her and ensuring her safe passage to the afterlife. The tomb is laid out like a house, with many chambers, to make her feel at home. I laid her body to rest in a sarcophagus of red granite. In the last chamber, Nefertari is pictured with the god Isis, who is giving her an ankh, and with it eternal life.

The afterlife

A tomb is called the House of Eternity because Egyptians believed that after death they would journey to the afterlife, a heavenly place with a heavenly River Nile. Bodies were mummified so they could be used again. This was why Egyptians filled tombs with furniture and everyday items.

The ankh is also known as the key of life. For Egyptians, this special cross was a symbol of eternal life.

Becoming a god

I am 51 years old and have just enjoyed my first Sed Festival. This is celebrated after a pharaoh's first 30 years of rule, and then every three years thereafter. Representatives from all over Egypt came to worship me and to celebrate. I presented offerings to the gods and was crowned, first with the white crown of Upper Egypt and then with the red crown of Lower Egypt. Finally, I ran between two points, symbolizing the borders of Egypt, in a ritual to reinforce my power over the whole kingdom.

Many representations of the Sed Festival show the king running alongside a bull to prove his fitness to continue to rule.

Ritual murder

The Festival of Sed was meant to renew a ruler's strength and energy. It probably replaced an ancient ritual of murdering pharaohs after 30 years when they were considered unfit to reign.

Here the gods are shown adoring Ramesses the Great at Abu Simbel.

Coming to the end

Since that first Sed Festival, I have celebrated 13 more and outlived many of my sons. My 13th son, Prince Merenptah, will be the next pharaoh. He is much older than I was. He thinks I have spent too lavishly on temples, but I know I have led a successful empire for 67 years. Now I am tired and in pain and do not fear death. I will be reunited with Nefertari in the afterlife...

Merenptah

Merenptah was almost 60 years old when he became pharaoh in about 1213 BC. Ramesses had neglected his army in later years. But Merenptah proved himself a skilled warrior when he fought the Libyans and the Sherden pirates again, killing nearly 9,400 of their men. He ruled for about ten years.

Ramesses' legacy

Ramesses was 91 years old when he died – an amazing age at a time when most people died before they were 40. The Egyptian people were struck down with grief. Few of his subjects had known any other ruler, and many thought the world would end without him. During the three-week journey from Pi Ramesse to his tomb in the Valley of the Kings, thousands of people crowded the banks of the Nile. They filled the air with sounds of crying and wailing, and women threw sand over their heads and tore at their clothes in grief.

This is the tomb of Ramesses II. For 50 years after he died, Egypt remained a peaceful and powerful empire, ruling many nearby states.

A legend lives on

Ramesses' legacy didn't last long. New enemies were attacking all the time, and less than 150 years after Ramesses died, his descendants lost their power and the empire he helped to build came to an end. However, thanks to his many temples and monuments, Ramesses II lives on as he always wanted to. These attract thousands of visitors every year, and over 3,000 years after he died, millions still know the name of Ramesses the Great!

These are the mummified remains of Ramesses II.

The real Ramesses II

Ramesses' monuments and paintings show him as the ideal king – tall, perfect, and forever young. His mummy reveals a man who was tall (about 1.7 metres, or 5 ft 7 inches), but who also had a long, thin, hooked nose and a long, narrow face with a heavy jaw.

Timeline

Fact file

The world of the ancient Egyptians is one of the most famous in history. There had been two separate kingdoms along the River Nile in Egypt, ruled by different kings. The kingdom in Upper Egypt was known as the white crown and the kingdom in Lower Egypt was called the red crown. In about 3100 BC, Menes, the pharaoh of the north, conquered the south and united Egypt. The united Egypt lasted about 3,000 years and there were about 170 pharaohs altogether. Successive pharaohs conquered other countries and established an empire.

The three Kingdoms

We divide ancient Egypt into three main periods: Old Kingdom, Middle Kingdom, and New Kingdom (separated by some short periods). During the Old Kingdom (2575 BC–2130 BC), pharaohs were buried in pyramids. During the Middle Kingdom (1938 BC–c.1630 BC), instead of being buried in huge pyramids, pharaohs were buried in underground tombs. Ramesses II ruled during the 13th century BC, during the New Kingdom (1539 BC–1075 BC). The pharaohs of the New Kingdom were kings of a massive nation, and many remains of their tremendous works, temples, and fortresses can still be seen today.

Egypt conquered

In 332 BC, Alexander the Great conquered Egypt, and Egypt became just a part of the empire of the Greeks.

Write your own journal

Make your own journal and use it to record events from your life. Stick in photos, newspaper cuttings, plane tickets, or anything else that will help you to remember important or happy or special events in your own life!

1. Make it

Buy a set of sheets of good-quality scrapbook paper. It will make the book more interesting if you select a variety of different colours. If you choose a large size, you will be able to put more pictures and words on a page. Choose plenty of sheets to make lots of pages. The best way to put all the pages together is to make holes in one side using a hole puncher and then tie them together with some ribbon or string.

2. Cover it

Before you tie your pages together, make a cover. Choose two pieces of coloured card the same size as your book pages. Decorate the front cover with a title and perhaps your name and some pictures. You could laminate these pieces of card to make the cover even stronger before you attach them to your journal.

3. Decorate it

The best journals are colourful and interesting. You could decorate the borders of each page by drawing a design around the edges, or gluing stickers, buttons, or anything you like to them. You could also add titles and lettering to the beginning of each page.

4. Fill it

Now you can write in or stick pictures into your journal. You could put pictures, programmes, and maps on one side, and write diary-style entries opposite these, or mix up the images and words on every page. Be creative and have fun!

Glossary

ankh symbol of life rather like a Christian crucifix, or cross

channel ditch or canal usually dug by people to re-route water, for example from a river to fields of crops

chariot horse-drawn, usually two-wheeled, carriage for transporting one or two people. In the time of Ramesses, chariots were well established as weapons of war as soldiers could use powerful bows while riding them.

concubine in ancient times, a woman who is allowed to live with a man and have his children but who is not married to him

crop plant such as wheat grown for food

delta wide, triangular area of damp land at the mouth of a river

embalmer person skilled in ways of preserving human bodies after death, such as using herbs and minerals

granite type of grey volcanic rock containing small crystals, which is difficult to cut and carve but is strong and hardwearing. Granite is often used to make monuments.

inscription written piece meant to last a long time, often found carved on graves and memorial structures to record or celebrate the achievements or life of a person

papyrus type of tough fibre from marsh plants woven into a paper-like material used for writing and drawing on in ancient Egyptian times

pharaoh Egyptian ruler in ancient times. The first pharaohs of the whole of Egypt ruled from around 3000 BC.

priest person with the authority to carry out religious ceremonies and act as a link between people and gods

quarry place where large amounts of useful stone are dug out of the ground

sarcophagus decorated stone coffin that a dead person is buried in

scribe person who writes records by hand

sedge grass-like plant with triangular stems that grows in wet ground

status position of a person in society or by law

strategy skill of planning movements and tactics in a battle

tax money that people have to pay to their rulers or government

tomb large grave, usually below ground in ancient Egypt

Valley of the Kings large cemetery or burial place for pharaohs, which is located near the ancient Egyptian city of Thebes (now Luxor)

Find out more

Books

Ancient Egypt (Explorers), Jinny Johnson (Kingfisher, 2013)

Ancient Egypt (Great Civilizations), Kathleen W. Deady
(Capstone Press, 2012)

Ancient Egypt (Pocket Eyewitness), (Dorling Kindersley, 2012)

Encyclopedia of Ancient Egypt, Gill Harvey and Struan Reid
(Usborne, 2012)

The Egyptians (Project History), Sally Hewitt (Franklin
Watts, 2013)

Websites

www.ancientegypt.co.uk/pharaoh/story/main.html
This British Museum website has information about the battle
of Kadesh and images from that event.

**www.bbc.co.uk/history/ancient/egyptians/launch_gms_
mummy_maker.shtml**
Test your skills as a mummy maker!

**www.childrensuniversity.manchester.ac.uk/interactives/
history/egypt/**
There's lots of information about different aspects of ancient
Egypt on the Children's University of Manchester website.

www.pbs.org/empires/egypt/newkingdom/ramesses.html
Visit this website for more information about Ramesses II and
ancient Egyptian society.

Places to visit

British Museum
Great Russell Street
London
WC1B 3DG
www.britishmuseum.org
An imposing stone bust of Ramesses II presides over the
Egyptian sculpture room and many other Egyptian artefacts in
the British Museum.

The Manchester Museum
The University of Manchester
Oxford Road
Manchester M13 9PL
www.museum.manchester.ac.uk
Visit the Ancient Worlds gallery at the Manchester Museum to
find out more about ancient Egyptians.

Louvre Museum
75058 Paris
France
www.louvre.fr/en
If you go to France, you could visit the Department of Egyptian
Antiquities, in the Louvre Museum, which includes a colossal
statue of Ramesses II.

The Australian Museum
6 College St Sydney
NSW 2010
Australia
www.australianmuseum.net.au
There are galleries of Egyptian paintings, sculpture,
hieroglyphs, pottery, jewellery, and architecture at The
Australian Museum.

Index